A Diamond in the Darkness

by

Veni Raj

Illustrated by
Tushar Kanti-Paul

GEORGE RONALD

OXFORD

GEORGE RONALD, Publisher
46 High Street, Kidlington, Oxford OX5 2DN

ISBN 0-85398-161-2 Softcover

Set by Sunrise Setting in Times 15 on 17 point
Printed in Great Britain

UP in the Diyang hills of Sarawak, on the Island of Borneo, there lives a boy called Liaz. Liaz was born in a longhouse. A longhouse is a great big house with many families living together. Liaz's longhouse has twelve families. Though they are twelve different families living in twelve different rooms, they live just as if they are one big family. If there is a marriage celebration in one family, it becomes a responsibility of every family in the longhouse. All the families will share the expenses and work to celebrate the marriage. Such unity always brings happiness to the children and the people of the longhouse.

Liaz comes from a race called the 'Land Dayaks'. These people usually live in the heart of the jungle or on top of the hills to protect themselves from their enemies. Liaz was born and grew up like any other Dayak child in the longhouse. He enjoyed playing among the

coconut groves, chasing butterflies and
splashing through the water in the nearby river,
and most of all he liked to go hunting for wild
boar. One day Liaz, his friends and some of the
older boys from his longhouse brought home a
wild boar and everyone had a feast.

Unfortunately Liaz and his friends did not
go to school for they did not have a school in
their village. The schools were very far from his
village. People in this jungle did not understand
the need for schools. They were farmers and
hunters and their sons did not need to go to
school to learn farming and hunting, for their
fathers taught them these skills. As Liaz was a
boy, it was the wish of his parents that he
should become a good farmer and hunter as

well. Every morning Liaz, who was only eight years old, would walk with his parents to the farm which was about two hours distance from his longhouse. He would carry the basket on his back which contained their lunch and enjoyed tramping along the narrow path of the rice fields. Liaz was very happy with his farm life. He was a helpful and obedient child to his parents.

Beneath this happiness something secret was happening to Liaz's life. Neither he nor his parents were aware of it. Slowly, slowly, slowly the vision in his eyes was fading away. He paid no attention to the dimness of his sight and he did not speak of it to his parents, so they did not know of the danger that lay ahead for Liaz. Several months passed by and one morning Liaz woke up in complete darkness. He groped around and stumbled and fell over on the floor. He called for help and started crying 'I can't see, I can't see. Mother, mother I can't see.' His mother, who was preparing the breakfast in the kitchen, heard him cry and came running to her son's call. 'What has happened to you, Liaz; what has happened to you, son?' she said. 'I can't see, mother, I can't see, everything is dark, I can't see.' His mother was so shocked she could not speak. She ran to her husband who

was at the riverside having his early morning wash. When he heard the news from his wife, he quickly ran to the house. In no time all the neighbours were around Liaz and his parents. They could not believe that he could become blind overnight. Most of them did not go to their farms that day. The chief of the longhouse went to call a 'bomoh' – a village medicine man.

The 'bomoh' performed a ceremony by burning some incense and he mumbled some words. Then he asked Liaz's father to bring a live chicken and a basin of water, which was placed in front of Liaz. The 'bomoh' looked into the water in the basin, closed his eyes and chanted a few Dayak prayers. Everyone around him also joined in the prayers by closing their eyes. Then he told one of the men to beat the drums as he killed the chicken in front of Liaz. He took a little bit of the blood and smeared it on Liaz's eyebrows. The 'bomoh' turned to Liaz's father and said, 'The evil spirit has taken away your son's eye-sight. It will give it back soon.' The Dayaks believed and hoped that by offering the life of the chicken the evil spirit would go away and Liaz's sight would return.

Many days passed by. Liaz's parents and neighbours eagerly waited for some change to take place, but nothing happened. They were worried and finally they decided to take Liaz down the hill to another doctor. As this was only a small clinic the doctor could not treat him, but told the parents to take Liaz to the big hospital in the capital city. The capital city was very far from his village. It would be a long and expensive trip for Liaz and his parents. All the families in the longhouse collected money and food for the trip to the big city. When finally they reached the city hospital, they were taken

to the eye specialist. The eye specialist checked
Liaz's eyes carefully and said, 'This boy needs an
immediate eye operation. Unfortunately we do
not have the facilities to treat him here. You
must take him to Singapore.' 'What! What!
Singapore! What is Singapore?' said his father.

The specialist gave him a queer look and said,
'Well, Singapore is in another country, and you
have to go by aeroplane.' On hearing such
words his parents gave up all hope. It would
cost a lot of money to go so far and they were
very poor farmers. Even if the whole longhouse

7

were to get together, they would not be able to raise such a large sum of money. They started back on their journey to their village, with broken hearts and broken spirits. By the time they reached the longhouse, they had already forgotten the words 'Singapore' and 'aeroplane'. They had never heard such strange words in their lives.

Poor little Liaz was now thrown into the world of darkness. He was so angry with himself. He felt like tearing the world apart. He could no longer see the colourful butterflies. He could no longer go hunting for wild boar with his friends. He could no longer tramp in the rice

fields and he could no longer see the rainbows
or the silvery moon at night. He would no
longer see the difference between the night and
the day. He would have to learn to live with
only one colour – black. Liaz's sorrow lasted for
many months. Then slowly he began to learn to
listen to the sounds around him. He would

listen carefully to the twittering of the birds; to
the wind blowing; and to the sound of the
dancing leaves. Liaz had always been a helpful
child. Even in this blind state he began to find
ways and means to help his parents. He decided
to chop wood for the fire and catch fish for

dinner at the river near by. He also learned a new thing. He learned to sing.

Several years passed by and Liaz grew into a youth. He often felt lonely. His friends could not be with him for they were busy with their hunting and farming work away from the longhouse. Catching fish and singing to himself were not really enough. He began to understand that the only way he could make himself happy was by making others happy. He found company in the little children that were growing up in the longhouse. Children were his best friends now. They followed him around and enjoyed the songs Liaz sang for them.

One day a great thing took place in their village. Some people from down the hill came with a Great Message. They were Bahá'ís. Now nobody had heard the name 'Bahá'í' in this longhouse. That night the longhouse families gathered. They listened carefully to the Message these Bahá'ís brought with them. As they listened with open hearts, they began to feel very happy. After a long meeting they decided that they too wanted to follow the Great Teacher Bahá'u'lláh and to call themselves Bahá'ís. Liaz, who was seventeen years old then, was curious to know about this thing

11

called Bahá'í. He listened very carefully to the
words which the Bahá'í teachers were saying.
His longhouse people were very happy to
become Bahá'ís. They were happy to learn
about the one true God and His goodness so that
they no longer needed to fear or worship the
spirits they thought lived in the forests.

All the neighbouring villages who had a
different religion used to make fun and laugh at
them for not having a place to worship in, like a
church. One day the chief told his people: 'It is
time now that we build a "church" to show our
friends in the next village that we also have a
place to worship.' A few months later they

started to work on the new building. They
chopped down some trees in the forest, and
with some nipah leaves as the roof, they built a
beautiful house, and they called it 'Bahá'í
Centre'.

Now they wanted to have a grand
celebration, so the chief of the house went to the
city to invite the Bahá'í people for the opening
ceremony of their Bahá'í Centre. As the Bahá'í
friends from the city were going up the hill,
they could hear from a distance the sound of the
drums and the gongs, the laughter of the
children and women. Everyone was busy. They
were dressed in their best clothes. As the Bahá'ís

from the city arrived, all the people in the
longhouse lined up in two rows and sang
'Alláh-u-Abhá' to greet them. Then they
brought a pig, slaughtered it in front of their
new building and sprinkled the blood in four
directions, as this was a custom among the
Dayaks. The new Centre was opened, they sang
and they danced the whole day and had such a
great feast. Everyone was so happy, that they
never had been so happy before.

As time went on the people in neighbouring
villages became very curious about this Bahá'í
longhouse. They saw that people from different
countries sometimes came to visit this house
even though the journey was difficult. But the
people in the neighbouring villages, who had

long had a religion of their own, had no visitors
from other countries. They wondered what
secret the Bahá'í longhouse held, and were not
very happy about it. Meanwhile the new Bahá'ís
eagerly awaited the visit of Bahá'í teachers.
They wanted to know more about their new
religion and tell their neighbours about it. The
only way they could learn about it was through
the Bahá'í teachers, for they did not know how

to read and write. Unfortunately the Bahá'í
teachers could visit only once in a while because
of the great distance and the difficult journey to
reach the village.

Liaz, who was very proud of his new
religion, wanted to tell all his friends in the
neighbourhood. Most of all he was happy that

he had found 'Someone' to talk to in time of
loneliness. Now he knew that there is Someone
very Great to help him in time of need and to
guide him to the right path. Whenever a Bahá'í
teacher came he would sit and listen carefully.
He learned prayers by heart and would beg the
Bahá'í teacher to tell him more about
Bahá'u'lláh. One night, after hearing the stories
about Bahá'u'lláh, he could not go to sleep. He

was so carried away with the love for his new
religion. He loved Bahá'u'lláh so much that he
wanted to tell the Great Message to the people
all over the neighbourhood or if possible the
whole world. Suddenly remembering that he
was blind, his heart broke and tears ran down
his cheeks. He whispered some words: 'How
can I serve Thee? How can I serve Thee? I am
blind and I did not go to school. Who will listen
to me? Nobody will listen to me.' He sobbed
and sobbed. Liaz was such a humble and
obedient person, God loved him very much. He

did not know what great plans God had for
him.

The next morning Liaz attended to his
chores as usual. He sat by the river bank, and as
he was fishing he thought about those great
things he had been thinking about last night.
Suddenly he was awakened by the sounds of the
children who were running towards him calling
his name. Children were his best friends and he
loved these children very much. Quickly an idea

came to his mind. 'Children!' he said. 'That's it! Children! First I will teach them all that I know. I will teach them songs.' In his excitement he threw the fishing rod aside. He collected all the children and took them to the Bahá'í Centre. He started his first lesson, prayers and songs. The children were so interested in his prayers and songs that every day they would attend his class without fail. Apart from this, Liaz also encouraged the children to go to school. Very soon the Government was going to build a school in the neighbourhood and all the children could go to school. He knew now how important it was to go to school. Liaz became a strong 'pillar' in the community. He was not only a teacher for the children but also a teacher for the parents. He always reminded the parents

of Bahá'u'lláh's teachings that education is important for all.

Now Liaz was no longer satisfied with just singing words and telling stories. He realized that something else was really missing. He wanted to play music. He knew that music would enrich his songs and make the children's class more lively and joyful. It had been a childhood ambition to have a guitar of his own, and he wanted a guitar so badly. He had seen a guitar when he was a small boy when he went to the city with his father. He had always longed

to have one of his own. To buy a guitar would cost a lot of money. He did not have much money and he knew he could not ask his parents, who were too poor to afford such luxury. He did not wish to trouble his friends either, but he knew that he could rely on the One Who always answered his needs, that One

God Who loved him and helped him whenever
he was in trouble. Liaz prayed to God with all
his heart one night, to show him the way to
achieve his desire. After a few days of praying
and thinking, he had an idea. 'Why don't I make
a guitar for myself? There are lots of trees in the
forest and I know how to cut them down.
Maybe the children can help me.' He sat down
immediately to think of ways and means to
make a guitar. He still remembered what a
guitar looked like.

He worked for a long time. First he had to cut the wood with a saw to the right size, and then he had to carve it into shape with the help of the children, which took him several weeks. Though he made several mistakes, he did not give up. After that he had to sand the pieces to make the surface smooth. Many times he felt

with his hands to feel whether the shape was
right and the surface was smooth enough. He
sanded them again and again and again until he
was satisfied. Then he joined all the pieces
together very carefully with nails. Many times
the hammer slipped and he hit his fingers. When
the guitar was almost ready, he found he still
had to make many adjustments to the wooden
pegs he had fixed on the guitar.

The work was done. At last the guitar was
ready for use. His patience and long hours of
work had produced a masterpiece. The children
were immensely excited about the new guitar
and they were so proud of their teacher. His
parents were overjoyed to see what had been

made by their son. They were happy that
blindness had not set him back in life, but
instead led him on to do great things. Liaz sang
to the hearts of many people. Whenever Bahá'ís
visited from a different region, he would come
with his little band of children and serenade the
Bahá'í friends with his own Bahá'í songs.

From singing Liaz turned to composing
songs. He found out that there were very few
Bahá'í songs in his language, so he began to
make his own songs with his own music.
Bahá'ís from other regions who spoke his
language would come all the way to learn the
songs from him, as his songs were sweet and
melodious. Even the children from the
neighbouring villages who belonged to another
religion would come to this longhouse, to listen
to Liaz's melodious songs. Liaz's desire to give
the Message in his region is now fulfilled. God
answered his prayers. Though living in
complete darkness he has become a shining
lamp giving light to the entire region.